This book may be intended for
kids, but you're young at heart
and the _bat_ on the leathery-
grained cover was irresistible.

So Merry Christmas, Ann

from Alpine

FLYING FUR, FIN AND SCALE

FLYING FUR, FIN AND SCALE

STRANGE ANIMALS
THAT SWOOP AND SOAR

BY MARY LEISTER

WITH ILLUSTRATIONS BY TONY CHEN

STEMMER HOUSE
PUBLISHERS, INC.

Owings Mills, Maryland
1977

Portions of this book were originally published in somewhat different form in *Ranger Rick's Nature Magazine*. The illustrations on pages 12, 14–15, 23, 28–29, 30–31 and 73 are reprinted from *Ranger Rick's Nature Magazine* by permission of the publisher, National Wildlife Federation.

Inquiries should be directed to
STEMMER HOUSE PUBLISHERS, INC.
2627 Caves Road
Owings Mills, Maryland 21117

A Barbara Holdridge book
Printed and bound in the United States of America
First Edition

Published simultaneously in Canada by George J. McLeod, Limited, Toronto

Library of Congress Cataloging in Publication Data

Leister, Mary.
    Flying fur, fin & scale.

    Bibliography: p. 83
    SUMMARY: Explains how animals other than birds fly and soar through the air.
    1.   Animal flight—Juvenile literature.
[1.   Animal flight]   I.   Chen, Tony.   II.   Title.
QP310.F5L44   596′.01′852   77–7620
ISBN 0–916144–07–0

To each and every one of my nieces and nephews—
with special recognition to the budding biologists,
Floyd Reeser and Gary Smith

ACKNOWLEDGMENTS

With special thanks to Helen Stackhouse, librarian extraordinaire,
and to Barbara Holdridge, for her vitality, her wit and her insistence
upon excellence—or as close to it as the fumbling writer could manage

CONTENTS

INTRODUCTION

Because, one spring morning, I found a little mound of feathers in the pasture fencerow, this book came to be written.

The handful of feathers, all of them gray and white, had covered a mockingbird's skin until, a few hours before, a fox pulled the bird from its roost in the honeysuckle tangle and ate it.

But before he ate it he pulled its feathers; and being neither hurried nor frightened, he did not scatter the feathers about but left them all together in a little round heap, so that when I found them they looked as though the mockingbird had just stepped out of them and gone for a bath.

Because the feathers were all there and the bird was not, I noticed the varied shapes and conditions of the feathers, and noticed how very different the soft, curved body feathers were from the stiffer, straighter flight feathers, and how much more fluffy and downy the short, inner body feathers were than the longer, firmer outer ones.

All these varied feathers from the body of one small bird piqued my curiosity and sent me to my books to learn just how complicated and intricate and fascinating ordinary feathers really are—and how indispensable they are to flying.

I learned that the soft and downy inner feathers keep a bird's body warm; that the resilient, finely curved outer feathers make a bird's body surface smooth and rounded, so that it slips easily through the air as it flies; and that the strong, bold feathers that edge the wings and form the tail have practically everything to do with a bird's ability to fly.

A bird's large structural bones are hollow, which considerably lessens the weight its wings must lift, and its powerful chest and shoulder muscles enable its wings to perform the strong, sweeping motions of flight. But that isn't enough. In order to fly, a bird needs its feathers.

The strong, bold feathers of a bird's wings and tail extend far beyond the bones and flesh of those organs and give the bird a wide extension of lightweight surface to carry its body in flight. Moreover, the flight feathers of its wings are designed with the leading edge of the feathers narrower than the trailing edges, so that, as the wing moves up and down and forward and back, a propellerlike action results. The bird is "propelled" in a forward direction.

Every individual flight feather is under the bird's control. The bird can pull groups of feathers together or spread them apart. It can twist the quills, open the barbs, or hold a single feather perpendicular to the extended surface of the wing or tail. A bird closes its wing feathers tightly and pulls with great force on the downward stroke, then loosens the feathers and lifts its wings with scarcely any effort at all, because the air goes through as easily as through a sieve.

But how, then, does a bat fly? I wondered. A bat has no feathers to extend its flying surface, no out-of-balance feathers to act as propellers, and its wings are made of fine, light skin through which the air cannot flow when the wings are lifted.

Flight upon wings without feathers is as much an art as flight on feathered wings. It, too, depends upon powerful muscles, upon delicate balances and superb control. Like wings with feathers, these wings of fine skin are curved and stretched and raised and lowered and turned and flexed and dipped and swerved, and all the minute spaces upon them are also individually curved and stretched and flexed and twisted in exquisite maintenance of balance and speed and control. They utilize the "lift" of the air as it passes over the moving wing and the flowing currents in the invisible sea.

A bat flies, I learned, as though it were swimming through the air. It folds its wings so there is little exposed surface as it raises them and swings them foward, then it opens them wide and pulls them, like wind scoops, forcefully back. The tips of its wings nearly touch as it brings them, folded, up over its back, and nearly touch again as, wide open, they sweep beneath its belly.

The wing bones of a bat are slender and hollow, and the spread of its membranous wings is vast in relation to its tiny body—a full-grown little brown bat may weigh only one-fourth of an ounce, but its wings will spread to seven inches. A bat flaps its wings, moves them through the whole swimming motion, from ten to twenty times in every second of its flight—all the while snapping up insects, evading its enemies, and manning its echo-location equipment to avoid slamming into treetops or other bats in the darkness.

From the study of bat wings I went on, then, to read of the fossil records of those ancient flying reptiles, the pterosaurs or pterodactyls, from ages long gone. I wanted to know more of them because they, also, flew without the aid of feathers.

They flew with great spreads of membranous skin stretched from the sides of their bodies to the outside toe of each front foot. These outside toes, called wing fingers, were greatly elongated, and they supported the end of the wing membrane as it was moved up and down by the widely extended "arms."

Some of these flying reptiles from 170 million years ago were as small as sparrows, while the largest we know of had wingspreads of perhaps twenty feet. Their bones were hollow, so that the body weight of even the largest was probably not great. An albatross of today, for instance, has a wingspread of eleven feet (approximately 3.3 meters), but it weighs only about seventeen pounds (8 kilograms).

It is possible that these winged reptiles of the Jurassic age went gliding through the air on rising drafts of wind beneath their outstretched sails of skin, but it is far more likely, from what is surmised of their habits, that they flew as the bat flies, by swimming through the air.

While I was engrossed in the study of the ancient flying reptiles, I stumbled upon a reference to flying reptiles of the present day that took me completely by surprise. Actually, it turns out, there are three reptiles—two kinds of lizards and one kind of snake—that sail through the air in a kind of parachute-glide, with nothing like the real flying equipment those ancient reptiles had. Today's flying reptiles are fairly obviously not descended from those early fliers, but they are far more intriguing because they are alive *today!*

Instantly fascinated, I set about trying to learn more about these flying lizards and flying snakes. I spent more than a year in library research, and found, to my delight, not only the flying reptiles, but flying frogs, flying foxes, flying lemurs and flying marsupials, in addition to the flying fish and flying squirrels I already knew about.

I found little information about any of these flying creatures in any one place. A reference here, an allusion there, a meaningful line somewhere else, and sometimes, but rarely, two or three whole paragraphs of real information in one blessed book.

But in the course of the year, I did learn that these little creatures which fly without feathers have their own special ways of feeding, of mating, of rearing their young, all adapted to this new dimension of transportation by air.

All of these animals soar through the air without the aid of feathers, but only the bats and the flying foxes truly fly—that is, they propel themselves through the air. Bats and flying foxes move their wings up and down and forward and back to bring about actual locomotion. They can move up or down or sideways while flying in the air, or they can turn around and go back to where they came from. They have full control.

But all the other "flying" animals—the fish, the frogs, the lizards, the snakes, the squirrels, the colugos, the marsupials—have learned only to soar from high to low, from up to down, from high in one treetop to low on the trunk of another more-or-less-distant tree, or down to the ground. They accomplish this parachutelike travel by spreading membranes, by making their bodies wide and flat, and then by sliding downhill on the resistance between the broadened body and the air beneath it.

It is interesting to notice that several species of flying fish, from differing genera, not closely related to one another, have developed shoulder fins as wide as wings and can escape from the water for brief intervals of flight through the air.

But among the amphibians, so far as I know, only a few frogs have developed enough webbing between their toes to balance themselves in the air, and all of these frogs are closely related to one another. They all belong to the same genus, *Rhacophorus*, and they all live in the same widespread but general tropical area, from southern China down the Malay Peninsula.

The three flying reptiles live, also, in the same general area, but the two kinds of lizards that are known to flit about among the tree limbs belong to two quite separate families. The lizards, of course, are not related to the flying snake, which, in any case, flies in its own distinctly different manner, without the spread of membranes such as the other creatures use.

When we come to the mammals, we find that three different orders—the squirrels, the flying lemurs (colugos), and the several marsupials of Australia all fly by means of a furry membrane stretched out from their bodies.

Flying squirrels are scattered all over the earth, but they belong to many differing genera. Flying lemurs all belong to the same species and are all closely related, although those in the Philippines differ slightly from those in Malaya, southern China and Indonesia. But the flying marsupials of Australia belong to three quite separate genera, and all three of them are more closely related to nonflying marsupials than they are to each other.

No one knows why all these vastly unrelated animals developed the same method of traveling through the air. No one knows how they all learned to fly. Perhaps *you* will be the naturalist who discovers the answers to these riddles.

June 1977 MARY LEISTER

FISH

FLYING FISH

Let's pretend we are aboard a small sailboat out in the blue waters of the Gulf Stream, just off the coast of Florida. A great school of flying fish, like a flock of low-flying swallows, is skimming and dipping above the rolling waves of the sea. Their broad fin-wings and filmy tails glitter like small rainbows in the sunlight. Their flight is so lovely that it is pleasant for us to think they are flying for the pure joy of spinning through the lightness and brightness of the sunlit air. And perhaps they *are* flying for practice. Perhaps they *do* fly just for the fun of flying—some of the time.

But, almost always, when these fish are out in the air above the water, we will see a school of dolphins out there, too, leaping after the flying rainbows, or else swimming rapidly beneath them, racing to catch up with them, to be ready to gulp them down when they eventually drop back into water. Sometimes the telltale fin of a shark cuts the water behind them, and sometimes the swirl and flash of a hungry barracuda can be

3

seen. Then, we know, the flying fish use their power to fly into the air because an enemy is chasing them from down in the water.

These flying fish, whether they are flying for fun or fleeing from their predators, swim as hard as they can, with vigorous thrustings of their fins and their tails, until they reach their top water-speed of twelve to fifteen miles per hour. Then they fold their fins tightly against their silvery bodies and burst like meteors through the surface film of the water. As soon as their shoulders are free of the water, they fling their fin-wings open upon the air, but still they hold their tails down in the curve of the sea, vibrating them at fifty times a second.

They skim along the top of the water at a splendid rate until they gather enough momentum to propel their entire bodies into the air. Then, supported by the spread of their wide fin-wings, they sail through the air for three or four seconds, gliding above the water for 150 feet or so. Their time in the air and the distance they cover depend upon the strength of that initial thrust out of the water—as well as upon the direction of the wind and such other weather conditions as storms or heavy rains, met in that fickle element, air.

At the end of each glide, the flying fish usually drop back into the water. Sometimes, with their wings spread to the winds, they just dip the lower lobes of their tail fins back into the crest of a wave and vibrate them like gauzy outboard motors until, once again, they have gained enough speed to send themselves skimming into the air.

It isn't too unusual for a flying fish to make three or four of these additional takeoffs. An occasional, very strong fish may make as many as ten takeoffs and fly for a quarter of a mile before dropping back into the sea. But the single glide on the single takeoff is the common rule.

Apparently flying fish can see very well in the air during daylight hours, for they rarely crash into anything on a daytime flight; but at night they often land on rafts or in boats or on the decks of ships as high as twenty feet above the surface of the sea. Many flying fish probably strike against the sides of vessels in the darkness and fall back into the water stunned or injured or dead, and are quickly eaten by other sea creatures feeding near the surface.

Most flying fish are natives of tropical and subtropical waters, although there are many of them along the American side of the Atlantic Ocean as far north as Maine. There is an especially great concentration of these picturesque fliers in the Gulf Stream where it curves close inland just off Cape Hatteras, North Carolina. If you sail in these waters you are almost certain to see a school of fish flying above the waves.

Flying fish feed upon the microscopic or almost microscopic animals that, along with equally microscopic plants, make up the teeming clouds of plankton in the waters of the earth. Plankton animals consist of protozoa that never outgrow plankton size and of those drifting minuscule eggs and larvae that, if they aren't eaten first, will someday grow up to be fishes and starfishes and barnacles and lobsters and many other kinds of sea creatures.

These swarms of living plankton do not always stay at the same levels in the ocean. During the day, as the intensity of the light and the heat increases, the plankton layer sinks lower and lower into the water until it is sometimes 150 feet below the surface. But at night it slowly rises until its upper levels lie in the very top of the ocean water.

The flying fish follow their plankton food up and down through the water, and, of course, the animals that feed upon the flying fish follow them. Now, if the flying fish are down fairly deep, there is a great immensity of water about them and they can dive or rise or drop off to one side or the other when a school of dolphins or sharks attacks them. But if they are feeding at the surface of the ocean when a school of dolphins comes up from beneath them, almost the only way they can escape is by taking to the air.

However, fish that fly during the daylight hours face an added danger of being captured by fish-eating birds like cormorants or ospreys. Perhaps it is better for the flying fish that their plankton food mostly moves to the surface at night, when the birds are asleep, even though there is the chance of crashing into a passing ship when they take off in the darkness.

All flying fish have firm, streamlined bodies. When they grow to adult size they range from six to eighteen inches long, depending upon their species. But no matter what species they are, they all have wide, winglike front fins placed high up on their shoulders right on a line with their large, round eyes. Their tail fins are strong and curved. The lower lobe of the tail, so important for takeoffs, is long and much enlarged. Some especially beautiful flying fish in the tropics have a second pair of broad winglike fins placed well back along their abdomens.

The tiny, glassy eggs the flying fish lay in the sea are as round as fairy marbles, and they float in dainty rafts at the top of the water, where they are in plain sight both from above and from below. These floating eggs are part of the plankton of the ocean, and thousands of them are eaten by sea birds and by most of the undersea creatures that rise to feed at the surface of the waters, including even the flying fish that laid them.

But other thousands of these eggs become caught in the jetsam of the sea or in floating masses of seaweed, and because they are hidden they are protected. Some flying fish lay eggs that have long tendrils curling from them. These tendrils catch easily on the rough edges of the jetsam or in the floating weeds, and the eggs are carried along with the weeds on the drifting currents and the vagrant winds.

When the tiny fish hatch from these eggs they are part of the plankton, too, and more thousands of them are eaten by all the plankton-eaters, while great numbers of them do live to grow up.

When they are babies, their tiny bodies are mottled with many colors. Some kinds of these little flying fish have long whiskerlike growths hanging downward from the tips of their lower jaws. Sometimes these whiskers are as long as the little fish itself. In some species, when the young fish has grown to be two inches long, its chin whiskers have grown even more than the fish, and they trail out behind it like antennae wires as it swims. These "whiskers" are called barbels, and they disappear when the youngsters become adults.

Young flying fish take to the air when they are quite small. They vibrate their wing-fins while they skim through the air as though they are trying really to *fly*. But when they become adults they hold their wings almost steady and simply soar above the water. As they rush through the air, the wind makes a rattling sound on the silvery scales of their bodies, and when a whole school is in flight, it sounds as though they were, in fact, all flapping their wings.

In the fresh waters of Africa and of South America, there are two kinds of small fish that actually do flap their wings when they fly, and some naturalists think they may be supporting their bodies as they do this. But, like the seagoing flying fish, they can only fly in a straight line. They cannot turn to the right or to the left, or turn themselves about, as birds and bats are able to do.

The flying hatchetfish (or flying characin) of South America makes a takeoff run over the surface of a river with the rounded keel of its tail fin immersed and its front wing-fins beating rapidly against the water. This fish is only one or two inches long, but its takeoff run may measure forty feet or more in order for it to fly above the water for five or ten feet. In flight, it beats its wings so fast that they make a buzzing sound in the air.

But naturalists have also seen some of these flying characins take to the air without a running start. They just leap from the water into the air and fly nearly the same distance they are able to travel with the long takeoff. Since they do not always need the takeoff run, perhaps their fast-beating fin-wings, helped by their strong muscles, do work to keep them in the air for their brief flights.

In many African rivers there are pretty five-inch butterfly fish that spend most of their time swimming and feeding near the surface of the water. Now and again, for unknown reasons, they spring into the air and glide, with their wide, fanlike front fins flapping up and down, for six feet or more before dropping back into the water. These fish have well-developed shoulder muscles strong enough to support their small bodies in short fin-flapping flights, but biologists are not quite sure that these fish are actually flying.

Nor is anyone sure that the flying gurnard "flies." This strange-looking fish has a short head protected by bony plates and spines, and a body that is heavy and squared off like a box. It scarcely looks like a fish that could fly, except that it has such extraordinarily large front fins. These fins are divided into three sections. The dark hind sections trail like a theatrical cape; the center sections are spread wide like wings for flying; and the front sections are free and divided into long rays.

These free rays it uses like arms and legs, standing on them, walking on them over the bottom of the sea, and digging with them to overturn pebbles and to probe the sand in search of food.

What does it do with the winglike parts? Some people say the fish flies or glides for short distances over the water surface and that this is how it got its common name, flying gurnard. Biologists say that its body is much too heavy even for its unusually large wings to support it in the air, and that, besides, it lives on the bottom of shallow seas and should have no use for flying.

But whether or not the flying gurnard ever flies, there are other creatures in the sea that do leap from the water and soar for many feet above its surface. Among these are several kinds of fish whose lower jaws are extremely long, extending far beyond the end of their normal-sized upper jaws. These fish are called half-beaks, and they are often seen streaking like airborne torpedoes above the surface of the sea.

There are, also, the famous flying squids, which, powered by their own strong jet-thrusts, propel themselves from the water and high up into the air, where they then glide for considerable distances before they drop back into the sea.

Probably the most spectacular of all the sea's flyers are the giant rays, whose flat bodies extend on either side, without any constriction or demarcation, into flat, triangular fins, so that they look like crude models of "flying wings." These giant rays break through the surface film of the ocean's waters and actually flap their great, fleshy fin-wings as they glide, but do not fly, for short distances in the open air.

AMPHIBIANS

FLYING FROGS

No member of the frog family has either feathers or wings; but several species of small tree frogs, whose habitat is the sultry forest range of southern Asia and its outlying islands, fly without these helpful appendages. These little frogs pull in their stomachs and arch their backs, spread out the thin webbing between their green toes, and go gliding down the air on the soles of their feet!

They don't glide far, perhaps thirty or forty feet at a time, but that is a great deal farther than they could travel in one ordinary leap.

There are nearly fifty species of flying frogs throughout southeastern Asia, down the Malay Peninsula, out onto the Spice Islands of Java, Sumatra and Borneo, and over into Japan. They all belong to the same genus, *Rhacophorus*. Some members of this genus live in Africa, but, surprisingly, they do not fly.

All of these flying tree frogs of Asia are "hunting frogs"—

that is, they do not as a rule sit quietly and wait for their insect food to come to them; they go about actively hunting for flying insects. They scare up insects from limbs and branches and among leaves, and then leap to catch one on the wing, even if the insects are flying directly toward them.

These flying frogs are brightly colored. They are usually a glistening green splashed or spotted with several shades of shiny brown, yet when one is sitting still it looks so much like a piece of moss-covered bark that it is almost invisible.

Since this is so, you would think that they would sit silently among the leaves and keep out of sight of the frog-eating snakes and frog-eating birds which are their predators, and that they would just catch the insects that fly unsuspectingly by.

But a flying frog is almost always on the move. In a tree, it hops about among twigs and branches and leaps upward from branch to branch or from limb to limb, catching and eating insects as it goes. When, by leaps and hops, it is high up near the top of one tree, it may decide to go hunting in another

tree close by. So it arches its small green body, spreads out the webbing between fingers and toes, springs into the air, and goes gliding out and down for twenty or thirty or forty feet, to land with scarcely a sound on a lower limb of the chosen tree.

All tree frogs have large flat disks, or toe pads, on the tips of their fingers and toes, but these gliding tree frogs of Asia have disks that are positively enormous in comparison with the small size of the whole frog. These disks are so large that when a flying frog skims through the air from one tree to another and happens to catch a twig with only one toe pad, it can hang on quite safely.

Little tubular glands keep these disks covered with a sticky substance, somewhat like glue or adhesive tape. The flying frog can, in fact, go straight up the side of a tree or walk on the underside of a limb without falling off. And it never leaves sticky footprints behind it.

The frog's bright eyes are large and bulging. They peer out from small elevations well above the top of its broad head, so that it can see in front, behind, above and to both sides of itself, all at the same time. It can see the smallest insects flying, close by, in all directions. It keeps a wary eye out for its enemies, of course, and it apparently judges distance with considerable accuracy when it leaps into the air and glides to a distant limb.

Perhaps the best known of these flying frogs is the Mount Omei tree frog, *Rhacophorus omeimontis*, of southern China. It is a small mossy-green frog with brown splotches on its back and on the upper parts of its legs, and each brown marking is splashed with spots of a darker brown.

The female of this typical flying frog grows to be a little more than three inches long, but the male rarely grows any longer than two inches. The male has large white disks, called nuptial pads, on the first and second fingers of each hand. With these he clings tightly to the back of the female during their mating.

At mating time these flying frog males gather on the banks of a pond or in the trees around it and call, as do male frogs everywhere, for the females to come and join them there. This flying frog's call sounds a great deal like the chirp of a cricket; and while one cricket call doesn't carry very far, a whole chorus of several hundred flying frogs chirping like crickets can make a small pond a fairly noisy place. At any rate, they chirp loudly enough for the females to hear the serenade. The females then come leaping and gliding from the forests to the ponds, to claim their singing mates.

Now, although they have, in true frog fashion, gathered at a pond, these mated pairs do not leap into the water, as other frogs do, to complete their mating and egg-laying there. These flying tree frogs build nests of foam in which to lay their eggs, and they build them in the trees overhanging the pond.

When the female flying tree frog has selected her mate from among the singers, the two of them hop out to the very tips of twigs hanging low over the pool of water. And there, among the leaves, they build their nest and lay their eggs.

First the female, with the male clinging to her back, produces a small amount of fluid. Then she or the male, or both of them, beat this fluid with their legs until it becomes a light and foamy nest of bubbles that clings to the leaves and twigs beneath them.

Onto this bed of foam the female then extrudes her mass of tiny eggs, and the male drenches them with his sperm. When all the eggs are laid the female expels more fluid over the top of the nest. Both the male and the female beat air into this fluid. They kick it with their legs until it piles up into a high, foamy, protective cover around the eggs. Then they pull themselves out of the sticky nest and go leaping and gliding away among the branches, hieing back to the forest again and leaving their eggs to take care of themselves.

The outside of the frothy nest soon becomes dry and hard, but the inner part that surrounds the eggs remains an air-filled liquid in which the tadpoles quickly hatch, often in less than a week. And not a single egg is eaten by a fish or a snake or a turtle or by another frog, because the eggs are safely encased in the tree nest, not left to float unprotected in the water.

By the time all the eggs have hatched, the liquid in the center begins to soften the dried foam of the nest and to seep through it. The lively tadpoles, wriggling vigorously inside the small enclosure, finally push a hole in the bottom of the nest. All at once they fall out through the opening and drop several inches or several feet into the water below.

And now the tiny tadpoles face the hungry fish and snakes and turtles and larger water frogs, and some of them are eaten, but not all of them. A great number of them grow larger and larger as tadpoles. When they are nearly full-grown they begin to change into tree frogs.

Tiny stubs of hind legs appear like little bumps under the skin on either side of their wavering tails. These tiny stubs grow longer and break through the skin. Tiny toes appear. The tadpoles at first just drag these small legs behind them. But as the legs thicken and begin to look like frog's legs, the tadpoles learn to kick with them and to use them in their swimming.

Now the arms, which all this time have been forming in the gill chambers, break through the skin on either side of the tadpole "shoulders." The whole tadpole begins to change shape, and the tail grows shorter and shorter as it is resorbed by the tadpole's body. Since the tadpole cannot eat during this stage of development, the tail becomes its food.

While this is going on, the tadpole's lungs develop, its gills disappear, and its intestines become shorter. At last the mouth begins to widen, so that it can be opened clear back beneath the eyes, and within the mouth a tongue develops with which it can catch insects.

Now the little tadpole-frog begins to eat again, but instead of dining on the tips of water plants and the tender green and brown algae on sticks and stones, it begins to hunt insects and all sorts of tiny animals living beneath the water.

Eyelids develop, and the eyes become large, bulging up over the top of the head. The tail stub disappears completely, and the tadpole is now a very tiny, very new little tree frog, with rather large feet and very large disks on its fingers and toes.

In just a little less than six weeks after all these tadpoles dropped from their nest into the pond, they are climbing out of the water and hopping up into the trees. They hop straight up the tree trunks and out along the limbs, and they scare up flying insects and catch them as they go.

Then one fine day, when they are high up in the tops of the trees, they apparently feel a strange yearning. They pull up their stomachs, they arch their small backs, they spread out the wide webbing between their fingers and their toes. Then, as though they had been doing it for years, they leap freely from their perches and slide out and down through the empty air on the wide-webbed soles of their new green feet.

Most flying frogs live and mate in the same manner as the Mount Omei flying frog, but, of course, every one of the forty-odd species looks a little different from every other one, and some of them behave differently.

A flying frog of the species that lives in Borneo, *Rhacophorus nigropalmatus*, glides through the air on webbed feet that are larger, when spread out for flying, than its whole body and head.

Another species, *Rhacophorus dennysi*, living in the jungles of southern China and in Malaya, is probably the greatest flier of them all. It is said to glide, not thirty or forty *feet*, but thirty or forty *yards* from one tree to another. This bright-green frog with dark polka dots on its back is worshiped as a god by many people of the area. On holy days one of these spotted frogs is carried about in procession in its own sacred chair. The chair is draped with cloth and garlanded with flowers in such a way that the flying frog cannot leap away or fly from the festivities.

Almost all the flying frogs construct tree-hanging foam nests, but in Sri Lanka the females of the species *Rhacophorus reticulatis* wrap their eggs in foam and then carry them around on their stomachs until the tadpoles hatch. And in Japan another species, *Rhacophorus schlegelii*, hides its nests in underground burrows, close beside water-filled rice paddies.

Each pair of these frogs apparently digs its own tunnel into the bank of a rice paddy. The tunnel starts below the surface of the water in the paddy and slants upward into the earth beyond. At the end of this tunnel, still underground, the pair build a foam nest and deposit eggs in it, in just the same manner as the species that build in trees. But after the eggs are laid and the foam nest is completed, the adult frogs leave the burrow by going down the slanting tunnel, right into the water of the rice paddy.

Tiny tadpoles hatch from the eggs they have left behind, and there the tadpoles develop into flying frogs, under the ground, in the foamy liquid of their nest. When they have all become fully developed flying frogs, they push through the softening sides of their dried foam nest, and then they, too, hop down the tunnel into the water. After a day or two in the rice paddy, they climb into the trees close by, and are soon gliding through the air from one tree to another, without instruction and without mishap.

REPTILES

FLYING LIZARDS

Millions and millions of years ago, when giant dinosaurs walked upon this earth, several of their reptile relatives learned, somehow, to fly. They had no feathers, but they had loose membranes of skin stretched from the sides of their bodies to the outside toe of each front foot. These outside toes, or wing-fingers, were so long that they supported the entire outer end of the wing as it was moved up and down by the arm over which it was stretched.

These prehistoric flying reptiles, so far as we know, actually flew above the earth and out over the shallow seas, by flapping their leathery wings with the aid of powerful chest and shoulder muscles. But these flying reptiles all became extinct. We don't know what happened to them, but we are fairly certain that the flying lizards of today are not descended from them, even distantly.

The flying lizards existing today do have loose membranes of skin extending from their bodies, but they have no wing-fingers and no powerful chest and shoulder muscles, so they

23

cannot flap their wings. They simply spread them out and glide through the air.

There are several species of present-day flying lizards, belonging to two different families. They all live in southeastern Asia, spreading down the Malay Peninsula and out onto the Spice Islands that stretch into the seas from the tip of that slender finger of land. It is the same general area that is also home to the flying frogs.

All of these flying lizards live in jungle trees, and they are all able to spread the membranes of their bodies and go gliding through the air like planing insects or like soaring birds. But they always glide downward from tree to ground, or from tree limb to tree limb, or from the limb of one tree to the trunk or limb of another. They never flap their membranes to move themselves through the air or to turn themselves about, and so, although we call them flying lizards, they really only glide and never truly fly.

The flying lizards with the fanciful name of flying dragons are delightfully nimble and fleet-footed little lizards. When they sit quietly upon a branch with their "wings" folded, they are almost invisible, for their satiny gray or brownish or greenish bodies are covered with spots, or else banded with dark wavy lines; and they blend so perfectly with twigs or with the roughnesses of the lichen-covered trees that they just disappear. One naturalist thought a small tree he was watching was empty, until he struck it with his hand—and half a dozen flying dragons popped off it. Their coloration is so perfect that even when they are running and jumping about on a branch you usually see only the motion and not the lizards.

But when an invisible flying dragon leaps into the air in pursuit of its insect prey, or when it glides from one tree to another, it spreads its wide gliding-membranes and instantly becomes as gorgeously colored as a tropical butterfly. The membranes it opens are brilliant orange, splotched or banded with shiny black. Its belly, now exposed, is pale yellow. Some of these lizards have dewlaps or throat sacs. In the male lizard of one species, the throat sac is orange with a spot of blue at the base. In the female, the entire appendage is sky-blue. It is no wonder that these flying dragons are also called butterfly lizards.

The butterfly wings of the flying dragons are like two layers of skin with five to seven curved, supporting ribs between them. These ribs are equipped with muscles that move the wings forward or back, opening or folding them, but never moving them up and down.

When a flying dragon is moving about in the trees, it keeps its gliding-membranes folded back against its body, much as birds carry their wings when they are not flying. When it leaps into the air, it pushes the rib supports forward to spread its butterfly wings, and it glides gracefully and vividly downward at a long angle, much farther than a simple jump would permit.

But none of this, neither the gliding nor the wing movement, is done in slow motion. A flying dragon on its feet is a scampering, skittering creature, and a flying dragon in the air flashes its wings forward so swiftly, and folds them back so quickly when it lands, that the human eye cannot really see it happen. We see neither the opening nor the closing but only the resplendent color of the gliding flight.

When flying dragons are full-grown they are from twelve to sixteen inches long, but their bodies are so slender and their long tails so delicately tapering that when their membranes are spread for flight they appear to be all wing.

When the female flying dragon lays her eggs each year, she deposits ten or twelve at a time. She buries them either in the soft, sawdusty materials in a rotten log or in the leaf mold of the jungle floor. Her eggs are only half an inch long, and they are oval-shaped, with soft, parchmentlike shells.

Two months after the eggs are laid, the baby dragons cut their way out of the eggs into the teeming life of the jungle. They are perfectly able to find their own food, to take care of themselves, and to glide tiny distances on their own little butterfly-colored wings.

The other flying lizard, the flying gecko, lives in the same steaming jungle lands as does the flying dragon.

The female flying gecko lays only two eggs in a clutch. She sometimes hides her eggs under logs or stones, but mostly she places them under loose pieces of bark on a jungle tree, or under a loose board on the side of a house. The gecko's adhesive toes allow it to climb up walls and tree trunks, and to walk upside down on ceilings or on the undersides of limbs, without danger of a fall.

The outsides of the round eggs are covered with a sticky substance, so that they adhere to whatever they are laid on or against. They can be placed safely even on the trunk of a tree. If both eggs are laid at the same time they will stick together, but they are usually laid a day or even two days apart—and they may be deposited right on top of another lizard's eggs.

After laying her eggs the female flying gecko goes off about her own business and pays no further attention to them. But it doesn't matter. Six or eight weeks later a fully developed little flying gecko cuts its way through the hard white shell with an egg tooth, which it later sheds, and steps out into the jungle world.

The baby gecko is very, very tiny, but it is perfectly able to look out for itself, and the first thing it does is to set about finding something to eat. Active and plucky, it tries to eat any insect that comes along. Sometimes it will attack an insect or a spider that is many times larger than itself. Sometimes it is successful, too.

But it has to eat large insects in small bites, because parts of the gecko's lower jaw, and the flying dragon's, too, are fused together, so that the mouth cannot be opened very wide. Like the flying dragon, the gecko has a thick tongue, wide and fleshy, fixed to the bottom of the mouth except for the front end, which is free and can be extended to capture insects. This type of tongue, however, is far less effective than the free, club-shaped tongue of the chameleon.

The little gecko, like all its lizard kin, has many enemies. It is hunted by snakes and by birds and by all sorts of carnivorous furry animals. Its best means of defense is to run away and hide. The gecko is particularly vulnerable because it has only a soft skin on its back. The teeth and claws and beaks of its enemies can easily penetrate this soft skin. If one of these enemies pounces upon its back and not upon its tail, its first capturing grasp is secure and the little lizard is quickly killed. This is probably one of the reasons why the gecko is usually active only at night. The flying dragon is much more secure. Its back is covered with heavy overlapping scales that protect it from the teeth and claws and beaks of its enemies. It usually remains active during the day.

A flying dragon's long tail does not break off easily, but if an enemy catches hold of a gecko's tail, the tail snaps off and the gecko runs to safety, leaving its tail behind. The tail will quickly be replaced by a new one, but this one will, most likely, be poorly shaped and even clumsy. But the gecko itself is still alive, evading its own enemies while capturing and eating many insects.

A gecko grows very fast. Only a few days after creeping out of its eggshell, it has to shed its skin for a larger size. The skin comes off in shreds, and the gecko sheds it over and over again during the first few months of its life. As the gecko nears adult size, it does not grow so fast, and so does not shed its skin as often. When fully grown the gecko will be only eight inches long, tail and all, and will shed its skin only two or three times each year.

The flying gecko has truly a great amount of skin to shed— not only its body skin but also the outer skin of the membrane that loosely encloses its entire body.

This gliding-membrane grows completely around the gecko's body. Only its head extends beyond it. On the front of its arms the membrane reaches between wrist bone and shoulder bone. It spans the gecko's sides between its arms and its legs. Even its fingers and toes are webbed like a frog's, and its tail has extra flaps along its entire length. When the flying gecko is prowling or at rest, it carries this skin in folds all around its slender, purple-brown body. But when the gecko decides to launch itself toward another limb or another tree, it stretches out both arms and legs, spreads all fingers and toes, holds its tail straight behind, and goes gliding through the air, using its own outstretched skin as a parachute.

FLYING SNAKES

In the same steaming jungles where the flying frogs and flying lizards live, there lives one of the most spectacular snakes in all the world—a flying tree snake. Its territory stretches across southeastern Asia from southern India into southern China, down the long Malay Peninsula, and out onto the wild and wondrous Spice Islands.

This flying snake is called the golden tree snake, although its body may be black or olive or green, and it may have ornamental markings in various designs in colors of yellow or orange or mauve or red. But regardless of all those varieties of coloring, it always has a black head, and its head is always decorated with golden-yellow spots, or crossbars.

The golden tree snake is about three feet long, delicately slender, and so light in weight that it slips like a shadow across leaves and the thinnest of twigs. When it is lying partially coiled and perfectly still, it looks like the tendril of a vine. It is one of the best climbers of all the tree snakes, for it can slither right up the wall of a house as easily, apparently, as it can run along the topside of a tree limb.

Not only that, but it can jump from one branch to another over a gap that is three or four feet wide, even if the second branch is almost directly above it. It does this by coiling up tightly on top of the first branch and then straightening out so fast that it actually throws itself onto the branch it wants to reach.

But the most extraordinary aspect of this remarkable snake is its ability to "fly." From a limb high in one tree to the lower limb of another, or even down to the ground, the golden tree snake glides through the air for distances of eight, or twenty, or 150 feet, dropping like a short, thin lariat, and so earns its other common name, the flying tree snake.

The snake does not simply drop off a limb and go plummeting through the air to land on whatever object happens to be below. The golden flying tree snake first determines exactly where it intends to land, apparently, and it has a definite procedure for getting there.

Inside its scaled and brightly colored skin it has more than a hundred fine, crescent-shaped ribs that hold its body in its cylindrical shape. When the snake gets ready to glide from one tree to another, it stretches out straight along a limb. Then, working its muscles and pressing against the limb, it rolls its ribs forward and pushes them outward until it is almost as flat as a ribbon. It then curves the edges of this ribbon slightly, making its undersurface concave, and slides off the limb. Now, holding itself quite rigid, it sails down through the air at a forty-five-degree angle, looking like a long, weighted leaf.

When it comes close to where it wants to land, it pulls up its head, curves up the front part of its body (perhaps by first raising its tail just a little, although observers do not mention any tail motion), and lands with a gentle thud on the chosen branch. Immediately it streaks away at incredible speed into the leafy twigs to flush out any lizards or small birds that may be hiding there.

This snake seems to have some way of guiding itself through

the air, for in the dim light of its jungle world it never strikes against a branch on its way down, and, so far as anybody knows, it never lands on the wrong limb.

The female flying tree snake lays her eggs in the rotting mold of the jungle floor, but she pays no further attention to her eggs or to the hatchlings, who take care of themselves from the moment they cut themselves out of their shells and slide away among the trees and bushes.

Is the flying tree snake poisonous? Yes, it is. But it is not as dangerous to man as a rattlesnake, because its fangs are mounted in the back of its mouth. There is a groove or canal in the teeth, and the poison flows into this canal and into the

snake's saliva. The tree snake has to chew on its victims in order
to poison them. The snake uses the poison to paralyze a captive
animal while squeezing it to death by wrapping it tightly in its
coils. It does not usually kill with its poison.

During the daylight hours the flying tree snake hunts quietly
along the shadowed limbs and branches and among the leaves
of the vine-shrouded trees. The hot, motionless air around it
hums with the drone of a million insects.

A little lizard with bright-orange spots on its skin darts along
a branch, intent on capturing one of those buzzing beetles. With
a lunge so fast it is only a blur, the flying tree snake grasps the
lizard's right front leg in its back-curved teeth and throws a

tightening coil of its own body around the small body of the lizard. The lizard flips its head and its three free legs in a frantic struggle to get away, but the snake holds on. It pulls its coils tighter, pressing the breath from the lizard's body, and begins to chew on the hapless lizard's leg, pouring in its paralyzing poison.

In a few minutes the lizard is dead, and the golden flying tree snake swallows it whole. It swings its wide mouth open as far as it will go and, by working the two parts of its divided lower jaw as though they were two arms pulling on a rope, slowly forces the lizard in.

The snake's supple body expands to receive the bright-spotted lizard, and digestion begins on the head before the tail is inside its mouth. In addition to lizards, the golden flying tree snake eats birds and large insects, as well as any little furry animals that happen to cross its path when it is hungry. The tree snake's gastric juices are so powerful that they dissolve all its food completely. Flesh, bones, teeth, spines, scales, fur and feathers—all are liquefied, giving the energy needed to propel the strange little snake on its daily gliding expeditions.

MAMMALS

FLYING MARSUPIALS

In the tall trees of Australia live several species of flying marsupials, primitive mammals that have a pouch on the abdomen in which the females carry and feed their babies until they have developed well enough to face the outside world.

The several species of flying marsupials in Australia are not closely related. They belong to three quite separate genera, but they have all developed the special talent of gliding through the air.

The members of each species have gliding-membranes that stretch along their sides and are attached to their arms and legs. With the membranes stretched out to their fullest extent they are all able to glide downward for considerable distances, from high in one tree to low on the bole of another. They all have opposable big toes, so that they can use their feet like hands in grasping and climbing. They all have the same enemies: owls, foxes, bush fires, barbed wire (on which they become impaled when they fly into it in the night) and man. They all sleep during the day and are active only at night. And they come in three sizes—small, middle-sized and large.

The smallest of these flying marsupials is a tiny brown creature, with white underparts, that weighs less than half an ounce. Its lightsome body is only three inches long, but its tail adds almost another three inches to its length.

This flattened tail has a fringe of fine hairs aligned on either side, and it looks so much like a feather that the little fellow is called the feathertail glider. This tail is a delicate-looking organ, but it is actually strong and muscular, and the feathertail glider uses it constantly, as a support among the branches and as a rudder and control for gliding about among the twigs and branches of the tall trees in which it lives.

The feathertail's fingers and toes are tipped with deeply scored pads that are almost adhesive, and its claws are long and sharp. It is well equipped for the acrobatic life it leads, leaping and climbing and gliding high above the earth.

The feathertail glider is a bright-eyed, mouse-faced, mouse-eared little marsupial that eats insects and insect larvae as well as flower nectar, and probably pollen and a few petals now and again.

Living in hollow limbs or in knotholes in eucalyptus trees, it makes round, ball-shaped nests of gum leaves or of shredded bark. Whole family groups live together as long as the nest will hold them all. One hollow limb nest was found to have sixteen gliders living in it, but knothole nests usually contain only the mother and her three or four babies.

The babies are carried and nurtured in the mother's diminutive abdominal pouch until they are nearly four months old. After they leave the pouch they still cling to her fur, sprawling over her back, for a week or two until they are completely able to look out for themselves.

The feathertail's gliding-membrane is only a narrow strip of soft-furred skin stretched along its sides, but it gives all the support this small creature needs as it skims from limb to limb.

Owls and domestic cats seem to be the most persistent enemies of these tiny treetop fliers.

The middle-sized flying marsupials are known as flying possums or flying phalangers, but they are commonly called sugar gliders or honey gliders. Actually, there are three species of squirrel-sized fliers in this group, all of them closely related: the sugar glider, the squirrel glider and the yellow-bellied glider. The sugar glider is the smallest of the three. The squirrel glider is a trifle larger and has a fluffier tail than the sugar glider, but these two animals look so very much alike and their diet and living habits are so much the same that they can be described together.

The sugar glider and the squirrel glider are about the size of a gray squirrel, or a little larger, and have soft and silky fur, light blue-gray above and white underneath. Their wide gliding-membranes are edged in white and trimmed with a line of striking black. Their sharp squirrel faces are striped and patterned in light and dark, and one dark stripe runs from nose to tail along the middle of the back. The tips of their tails are black.

They are extremely attractive little animals, graceful in their movements and endlessly active. They look sweet-tempered and innocent, but they fight viciously if touched (although they are easily tamed), and they actually seek out, attack and harass other small carnivorous animals as large as themselves.

They live high in the air in hollow tree limbs, where they

build soft, round nests of leaves. They gather the leaves with their front feet but carry them in their curled-up tails. These little gliders cannot sail through the air unless their tails are free, so they scamper along the limbs on their sharp-clawed feet when they are carting nest materials.

Both sugar gliders and squirrel gliders make a great deal of noise during their nighttime activities; they hiss, they moan, they grunt, they cry, they scream. When they are angered, either because of an intruder or for some other reason, their voices are said to sound like wheezy alarm clocks running down.

Both kinds of gliders are able to cover land distances of perhaps 160 feet in a single glide—if they take off from a very tall tree—but their average glide is well under one hundred feet. They have wide, full membranes stretched out from their sides, and they glide with sureness and agility among the great limbs of the forest and from tree to fairly distant tree. They climb these trees in a swift spiral, going round and round the trunk, tails streaming behind, so that they appear to be *flowing* up rather than climbing.

They dine on a great variety of things. Their diet includes insects and insect larvae, mice and small birds, buds and blossoms and flower nectar. They lap up tree sap from wounds in trees. They eat ripe fruits, and they also eat the aromatic gum that oozes from trunks, limbs and twigs of eucalyptus trees, even when it is old and hardened and they must patiently lick away at it.

At birth the babies (usually two, sometimes only one and rarely three) look for all the world like round, fat worms. They crawl into their mother's pouch and attach themselves to her teats. And there they stay, eating and growing, out of harm's way—and out of sight. The mother regularly washes her young with her tongue, holding the pouch open with her hands.

When the babies are about eight weeks old they move out of the pouch and cling to their mother's fur, but they still feed from her pouch. By the time they are four months old they are virtually independent of their mother, but they may continue to live in the home nest if there is room. Thus, some nests contain only the original mated pair with their newest babes, while other, larger nests may have as many as a dozen gliders of all ages living contentedly together, in spite of family quarrels.

The third squirrel-sized glider is known as the yellow-bellied glider. Its living habits are much like those of its two close relatives, but it is considerably larger than they, its coat is dusky brown and blackish instead of gray, and its underparts are an astonishing shade of orange-yellow.

It is a noisy fellow and can easily be located in the night by the sounds it makes. It has a varied vocabulary of shrieks and gurglings, bubblings and mumblings, hisses and moans. And its movements also produce distinctive sounds: its long claws rattle on the tree bark as it runs along the limbs high above the ground, and its spectacular glides always end with a distinct "clop!" on the trunk of a tree.

As it shoots down from the treetops with its long tail streaming out behind, it looks like a dark shadow in the night. Its average glide is from 100 to 120 feet, though it is known to make much longer ones.

Its food consists mainly of buds, blossoms, leaves and fruits, supplemented occasionally by insects, and it has been known to lick greedily at the hardened gum of the eucalyptus tree for an hour at a time.

This middle-sized glider is as agile as a monkey in the treetops. It clambers out to the twigs where the flowers bloom, hanging upside down like a sloth, and bobs about, with its tail waving gaily behind, as the branches sway beneath its weight.

It is a gentle and placid creature, even when captured, and when feeding in the wild it carries on a snuffling conversation with its mate or with other family members in nearby trees.

Then there are the greater gliding possums. Usually called simply greater gliders or dusky gliders, they live in the sparse eucalyptus forests of the hills and mountains of eastern Australia. Here, where the tall trees grow in thinly scattered ranks, their dark forms may be seen on a moonlit night swooping downward from the treetops to cover 300 feet or more in a single glide.

Sometimes the tree with the freshest blossoms or the most flavorsome leaves may be too far from other trees to be reached by gliding. Then the dusky gliders simply sail as far as they can and cover the remaining distance by clambering slowly and clumsily over the ground.

They feed exclusively on the tender leaves and blossoms of eucalyptus trees, but since there are many different kinds of eucalyptus (gum) trees, their diet is not monotonous. They are exceptionally fond of the peppermint-scented leaves of the narrow-leaved gum, and they stuff themselves with the blossoms of the manna gum when it is in flower.

Their long, fine and silky fur is usually a rich dark-brown in color, but it often varies from black to a smoky gray or creamy white. Many dusky gliders have white heads or white spots on their heads, while some are creamy white from head to tail.

They grow to be as much as five feet long, but twenty inches of this length is fluffy tail; and even a five-footer weighs only two or three pounds. They have big, round eyes and upright ears. They also have claws like heavy steel hooks on hands and feet, and the first two fingers of the hands are opposable to the other three. Thus the dusky gliders can securely clutch the branches of trees and easily gather leaves and blossoms; but they are almost defenseless against their enemies—larger owls, foxes that have been introduced to this region, bush fires, barbed wire (which causes an agonizing death) and, of course, man.

The gliding-membrane of the dusky gliders is unique in the world of gliding animals because it does not follow the usual pattern of rectangular webbing stretched along the body between wrists and ankles. Instead, it is a wide triangular membrane that stretches between the elbows and the outsides of the ankles.

Instead of extending their arms to fly, they fold them. They place their hands at the sides of their heads, and, with elbows akimbo and hind legs thrust out, they go sailing through the night air like so many small, swept-wing jet planes, their eyes glowing like jewels if anyone turns a flashlight upon them.

The voices of dusky gliders pierce the night with loud, gurgling shrieks that ascend sharply in tone and then end in a series of peculiar bubbling sounds; but they can and do speak more softly with one another in slow and repeated hissing calls.

Home is a hollow limb or a hole high up in a tree, where they live singly or in pairs. Some of the more comfort-loving among them bring in leaves for their beds, but most often no lining material is added to the hollow. They return to their homes each morning as daybreak approaches, or earlier if they have finished feeding. Gliding in to the home tree, they land with a thump well up on its side, scarring the bark deeply with their sharp claws. After a momentary pause, they gallop straight up the tree trunk to their dens, roll up their tails, and disappear inside. (They actually do gallop up the tree, using first both front feet and then both hind feet.)

Only one youngster is born to a pair of dusky gliders each year, usually in July or August. At birth it is quite undeveloped; its eyes do not open until it is well past six weeks old, and it shows no traces of fur until after its eyes are open.

Although it outgrows the marsupial pouch when it is about four months old, it remains dependent upon its mother's milk for several weeks, clinging to the fur of its mother's belly or her back, possibly going out with her on her nocturnal feedings. The mother glides through the air as usual while the little glider remains in her pouch, but it is not known if she ever glides with her youngster clinging to her back.

When the young dusky glider begins to eat solid food, its mother makes a careful selection of only the very tenderest of the eucalyptus tips and the most delicate of the blossoms for its feeding.

As soon as the young glider has learned to gather its own food it begins to wander off by itself, but it often lives in the same den with its parents until fully grown and ready to find a nest and a mate of its own.

FLYING LEMURS

In the lands where this little jungle animal is found—on the Malay Peninsula, throughout the tropical islands off its tip, and in the Philippines—the people call it either a colugos or cobegos, a kubung or kaguan. But in our Western world we call it a flying lemur, although we know it does not fly but glides, and although, in spite of a slight facial resemblance, it isn't a lemur at all.

Its scientific name, *Cynocephalus*, means "dog-headed," and, it was once given another name meaning "cloaked monkey."

It has been a difficult little animal for scientists to classify. Loosely, it seems to stand somewhere near the primitive lemurs, the earthbound moles and the free-flying bats; but it doesn't truly belong with any of them. Biologists finally decided that it just wasn't closely related to any other living animal, so they put it into an order all by itself, the Dermoptera, which means "skin-winged." Yet we still continue to call it the flying lemur.

The size of a small cat, it is long, thin and cleanly stream-lined, and so completely wrapped in its great flying-membrane that it is difficult to see just what its body looks like. But its head is free of the membrane, and it reminds people of a dog, a fox, an otter and, of course, a lemur.

The flying lemur has four equally long, slender legs, broad feet and a tapering tail more than half as long as its body. The typical adult is from eighteen inches to two feet long, has a ten-inch tail, and weighs about three pounds. Its fur is short and extremely fine; it is soft and silky to the touch, much like chinchilla fur.

The coloring of flying lemurs is quite varied, but the males are usually a brownish color and the females tend to be gray-ish. Their undersides are yellow or orange or reddish-brown, and lemurs of both sexes are splashed all over with silvery-white patches so that they may blend right into lichen-splotched trunks and limbs when they are hanging in a tree.

These little animals cannot stand completely erect but are always crouched within their great cloaks. For that reason they are generally awkward and clumsy on the ground, and even in a tree they climb slowly and move about in a poky manner. Some people report that they have seen them galloping over the ground, loping up tree trunks, and indulging in all sorts of agile activities among tree limbs, but that does not seem to be their usual habit. Perhaps its mood—whether it feels mopey or nimble—depends upon the individual flying lemur!

But there is no doubt that when, in the darkness of the night, one of them leaps from a treetop and spreads out its gliding-membrane, it becomes a creature of another world. For long and lovely moments it sails through the air like a free-spirited kite, and it lands with ease and precision on the trunk of a tree that may be more than two hundred feet away from its takeoff point.

The flying lemur apparently steers itself as it glides by lean-ing to one side or another as if it were on a bobsled. As it ap-proaches its landing spot it lifts its tail membrane. This raises the front of its body, puts a brake on its speed, and lands it—with a "plop!"—facing upward and grasping the tree trunk with its keen-edged claws.

For the most part, flying lemurs seem to make no sounds at all. But sometimes, while they are eating, they utter wild and rasping cries into the night. These may be alarm calls, but we cannot be sure of that. They may be simply a means of keeping in touch with others of their species.

The gliding-membrane that encircles the flying lemur's body is the largest such membrane among all the gliding mammals. This membrane is a double skin with rich, silky fur on both sides. It begins on the flying lemur's neck, extends down its arms, and stretches between every one of its ten sharp-clawed, even-length fingers. Like a wide fur cape it extends down the sides of its body, along its arms and legs, and between the five knife-edged toes on each hind foot. It even envelops the long tail clear out to the point.

Taking proper care of this gliding-membrane is a prime concern for a flying lemur. When it is feeding or moving about in a tree, it keeps this furry membrane pulled tightly under its front legs so that it does not catch on twigs or branches. This, of course, is why, at least most of the time, it climbs and moves about so slowly and so carefully. When the flying lemur drops waste materials from its body, it hangs from a tree limb by its arms and daintily lifts the tail membrane out of the way so that it does not become soiled.

Flying lemurs usually sleep in trees that are quite some distance away from the trees in which they feed, although the trees in both areas may be the same species. All day long the lemurs hang among the branches of their bedroom trees, sound asleep in the leafy shadows. They usually hang by their arms, head up, but sometimes they hang by their legs and sleep head downward, like bats. Sometimes, too, they sleep while hanging horizontally, like sloths, with their arms and legs wound about a tree limb and their thin, membrane-wrapped bodies hanging below.

When darkness falls, the flying lemur awakens, preens itself to a silky sheen, and then climbs up among the highest limbs of its bedroom tree. From this high point it leaps into the evening air, opens its expansive gliding-membrane, and makes a long, spectacular glide to the lower trunk of another tree a hundred or more feet away. Immediately it climbs to the top of that tree and glides off to the next one.

If there is no other tree within two hundred or so feet of the one it is in, the flying lemur will fly as far as it can in one glide, land upon the ground, and walk in its clumsy-looking crouch until it reaches another tree. It may make half a dozen or more flights before it reaches the tree with its favorite leaves and blossoms growing upon it.

As soon as it arrives at its dining tree, it climbs up among the leaves and begins to eat. It climbs carefully among the branches, membrane properly folded, pulling the food toward itself with its hands and biting off leaves, flowers and fruit as soon as they are close enough to be reached by mouth. The flying lemur feeds in this manner until the dawning hours, and then repeats its long series of gliding flights all the way back to the bedroom tree for a long day of sleeping.

It would seem that, with such an extensive, thin membranous surface extending from its body, the flying lemur would need to drink a great deal of water, but not one has ever been seen at a watering place. So far as we know it gets all the moisture it needs from the leaves and blossoms and fruits it eats. It probably licks extra raindrops and dampness from other leaves, also. And perhaps the folding of the membrane about the body except during actual flight reduces the loss of moisture.

The flying lemur's body seems to be specifically adapted for the eating of leaves. It has a large stomach that is divided into two parts for the special digestive procedures that are needed, and its intestines are unusually long, apparently to allow time and space for thorough digestion of the rough material.

The front teeth in its lower jaw are divided into "combs." Each single tooth has as many as twelve comb-teeth growing upward from it. These comb-teeth scrape and shred the leaves into finer material for digestion by the stomach. They are excellent tools, too, for grooming its excessively fine fur, which requires a great deal of attention.

Flying lemurs mate during the winter, which, in those tropic lands, is not a severe season; and their babies, scarcely more developed than newborn marsupials, are born in the spring. There is usually only one baby at a time, but sometimes twins are born. The baby is blind at birth, and its skin is pink and wrinkled and naked. It clings tightly to its mother's milk-providing nipple. The two nipples are so far to each side that they are almost in the mother's armpits.

Like the baby bat, a flying lemur baby clings to the mother's nipple or to her fine belly fur and goes sailing along with her on her nighttime glides. But when the baby grows too heavy for the mother to carry around, it is left behind in the bedroom tree.

Here, with no one to teach it, it learns to fly, all on its own. Night after night the young flying lemur practices its glides until it is old enough to eat the tenderest of leaves and blossoms and fruit and is able to go gliding off with its mother to find just such food.

BATS

Bats by the hundreds of species and bats by the millions of individuals flutter their dusky wings over all the earth, from the tropical jungles of the equator to the uneven fringes of the timber lines in both arctic and antarctic directions.

Bats are mostly small, mostly dark, velvet-furred mammals that truly fly. Their wings are thin membranes attached to body, tail, legs and arms, and finely stretched over a framework of delicate, drawn-out finger bones. Only their small, clawed thumbs are free of the membrane.

Every bat has true wings, and every bat flies where it wills—or where its search for food leads it—propelled by its own firm muscle-power. I cannot imagine any bat, if it were given the choice, willing to exchange its fine, thin, flexible skin wings for even the most splendid wings equipped with feathers. For bats enjoy the most perfect flying organs ever designed.

To fly, bats first raise their wings, half-folded, above their backs; then, with the wings fully spread, they bring them sharply forward and downward, sweep them backward and upward, and half-fold them again above their backs. This cycle, so smoothly executed, is repeated ten to twenty times in every second during a regular flight. They use their arms and legs, their hands and feet and, sometimes, their tails in this motion, so that they are actually swimming through the air, whether they are making an erratic, somersaulting maneuver or a long, graceful sweep toward the earth or toward the sky.

Bat wings are often described as leathery, but they are not. They are of soft, living skin, so elastic that it stretches far out upon the bones of the arms and hands when the bat is in full flight and folds in fine lines, softly and without bulk, when the bat closes its wings and plunges downward in pursuit of an escaping insect.

It is the bat's arms and hands that supply the propelling power to its wings. The arms are sustained by the great muscles attached to its capacious chest; and these muscles are powered, in turn, by the remarkably large, remarkably strong lungs and heart enclosed within that chest.

Much of the amazing flexibility of the bat's wings is owed to the extremely long, many-jointed finger bones, spread widely apart and embedded in the tips of its wing membranes. These finger bones open and close the wing tips, hold them taut, and adjust them with delicate precision to every twist and turn, to every rise and plunge, and to every varying current of air.

The legs help to spread and to tense the rear of the wings as well as the membrane stretched between the thighs—the interfemoral membrane, as it is called. The tail, if it is attached, also supports and helps to control this membrane.

When the interfemoral membrane is curved inward toward the belly, it forms a wind scoop that acts as a brake on the momentum of the bat's flight. It is also used as a net, for trapping more insects than the bat can catch with its mouth.

Not all bats eat insects. Some eat fruit, and some live upon pollen and nectar gathered from flowers. Some large tropical bats eat small animals, and some bats eat fish. (The fish-eating bats have unusually long legs and large, powerful feet, with claws like hooked spears on which they impale the fish they find near the surface of the water.) And then there are the vampire bats, several species of them, which feed on the blood of sleeping animals, lapping it up from the small incisions they make in the skin.

But whatever they eat, all bats have voracious appetites for food and water. Their thin-stretched wings, so large in relation to their bodies, steadily lose their body heat and moisture to

the air, and they must make up for the loss by eating and drinking in great quantities.

To conserve heat and moisture while they sleep, most of these bats, solitary hunters though they are at night, hang together in close-packed clusters with their fellows throughout the daylight hours. Bats at rest, awake or asleep, hang head downward for hours at a time, with their hind feet hooked to twigs or vines, or else to rocks or rough projections of walls and ceilings. Only for the purpose of dropping waste materials from their bodies do they turn themselves over and hang by their thumbs, with their heads uppermost.

Bats eat from one-quarter to one-half of their own weight every feeding night of their lives. Since the majority of bats in the United States weigh a great deal less than one ounce apiece, it may seem hard to believe that they make much of an inroad on the insect population. But there are thousands upon thousands of bats, and it takes an astounding number of insects to fill up even the smallest bat!

Bats drink great quantities of water as well. They usually go immediately for a drink when they leave their sleeping quarters each evening, and they pause in their feeding many times throughout the night both to rest and to drink more water. Flying just above the surface of ponds or pools or rivers or creeks, they lap up the water with their little pink tongues, making trails of tiny dimples as they go.

Bats are creatures of darkness. They fly in the dark. They feed in the dark. They capture even the smallest insects, such as gnats and mosquitoes, in complete darkness. They can do this because they possess the ability to hear the echo of their own voices as the sound rebounds from moths and beetles and owls, as well as from leaves and twigs and other bats.

Most of the voice sounds made by bats are too high to be heard by the human ear. Their echo-location squeaks are so high and so short that even when they are picked up on sensitive sound-detecting instruments each squeak is no more than a "click." But that short, high-frequency click has been measured at one hundred decibels. (A pneumatic drill, used on road repairs, makes a ninety-decibel sound.)

Reportedly, some bats can make more than two hundred of these clicks per second, but the average bat probably makes only between fifty and one hundred. Since the clicks are emitted on two wavelengths at the same time, for distant and for close echoes, fifty clicks per second is still quite a feat.

When they are resting, but not asleep, bats emit these clicks at a slower rate of about ten per second, checking, perhaps, against the approach of an enemy—an owl, a cat or a snake.

In order to keep up this continuous stream of high-frequency squeaks, a bat has to have a strong vocal apparatus, and that is why the muscles of its larynx are so powerfully developed.

For years, scientists in many fields have experimented with bats and their amazing capabilities. During these experiments it was discovered that when a bat's mouth was sealed shut it blundered about without any ability to guide itself in flight. However, when its mouth was left open and its eyes were covered, it could fly and feed without difficulty. Thus the scientists learned that those high-frequency clicks were bounced back from objects around the bat, and that the bat, hearing the sounds, could fly in the dark without striking anything. But when next they sealed both the eyes and the ears, the bat still flew without fumbling. Now, with its ears sealed, how did the bat "hear" those all-important echoes that kept it from striking a single obstacle in the experiment room? How could it avoid every attempt to capture it in a net?

Part of the explanation is that the ears probably were not completely sealed from those high-frequency sounds, that much of the vibration was actually penetrating the ears. But also, it is strongly suspected by scientists that more than just the hearing mechanism of the ears is involved in receiving and translating these echoes. They think it is probably done by a combination of bat senses and special organs.

The ear in many species of bats is equipped with a special process called a tragus (a leaflike flap of skin) that stands upright just inside the margin of the outer ear, directly in front of the external opening of the inner ear. In many of these same bats there is also a lobe-shaped formation of skin, called an antitragus, outside the margin of the ear just below the tragus.

Both of these processes, or formations, are, in some way, aids to the bat's hearing; and yet, if either is removed, or even both of them, the bat still safely flies. Additional research may someday provide an explanation.

Some bats also have intricate folds of skin, growing in various designs, around their noses. These folds are lined with fine, sensitive hairs. It is thought that these facial crests may, in some way, direct the course of the sounds the bats emit. They may also be perception organs responsive to the returning echoes.

And then there is the great spread of the thin membranous wings, filled with networks of nerves and blood vessels, and so delicately sensitive that they respond to the slightest pulsation of the air about them. Their tips are inches away from the facial crests and the ears, yet they never brush an obstacle in the path of flight. There is speculation among those who study the navigation of bats that the wings themselves may be receptive organs for the vibrations of the returning echoes.

But the ears are certainly intricately involved in the echolocation system, for it has been discovered that they close when the clicks are made, and that they open again for each echo. Two hundred clicks per second, two hundred ear closings, two hundred ear openings—all in the same length of time. How busy the brain of the little bat must be as it translates the myriad messages of its sensor organs into answers to the constant questions: What is it? Is it good to eat? Where is it? Which way is it going?

Most, if not all, of the bats of the United States mate in the late fall, but the sperm is held within the female bodies and conception does not take place until the bats begin to stir about in early spring. Because of this, almost all the little bat babies in any one colony arrive in April, May or June—all on the same day.

The incredibly tiny babies usually arrive singly, although some species have two, rarely three, in a litter. The young are received into the apron of the mother's inwardly curved interfemoral membrane or into one half-opened wing. They are blind, almost naked and helpless. They can only cling to their mother's fur and drink the milk from her tiny nipples.

At first the baby goes with the mother on her nightly hunts, clinging upside down to the fur of her stomach with its head hanging between her legs. But by the time it is two weeks old it has grown too heavy for the mother to carry, and she leaves it behind in the home roost.

By this time also, its eyes are open, and it crawls about on the ceiling or the walls or among the twigs or vines, exploring the cave or the attic or the vine-entwined tree that is its home.

Dozens of other little bats are left behind in the roost, too, and they soon begin to chase one another about. In the excitement, many a little bat goes thudding down to the earth or the floor below. On its way down, it flaps its wings frantically, probably breaking its fall; but it can only crawl slowly, with loud protests, all the way back up. The screeches and cries and angry protests of baby bats can be heard by human ears—and so can the shrieking and calling of the mothers when they return in the early morning hours and go about locating their own babies in all the scrambling hubbub.

After a few nights of accidental falling and frantic flapping of wings, the baby bats discover that they can fly. They drop repeatedly, catch themselves in midair, and then circle about in the darkness of their home roost on the thin membranes of their own tiny wings. And each one returns to its own perch whenever it chooses.

So quickly does a young bat become expert at flying that perhaps the very next night after its first attempt it goes out with its mother on a short practice flight. Soon after that, it becomes a full-fledged member of the colony. It goes out on the nightly flights; it learns to drink from the river or the pond while skimming just above its surface; and it learns to locate and to capture its own food.

When a young bat is scarcely more than four weeks old it is completely independent of its mother, except that it hangs itself up beside her in her group when it returns each morning to the home roost.

FLYING FOXES

Flying foxes are not foxes with wings. They are huge bats with bodies as large as those of small crows and with wingspans reaching to five feet or more. Their bodies are covered with dark-brown fur, sometimes grayish or blackish, with a yellow ruff across their shoulders that gives them the appearance of wearing a cape. They have very short tails or no tails at all.

They have small, pricked-up ears spaced well apart on their fine-shaped heads. Their eyes are large and brown and clear. The long, clean line of their muzzles combines with the broad

brow to give their faces a triangular and somewhat foxy look. Thus, because they look like foxes and because they fly, they are called flying foxes.

Flying foxes are the largest bats there are. They belong to a group of bats called fruit bats, which, as their name indicates, eat fruit instead of insects. Since they must have ripe fruit to eat all year round, they live almost exclusively in the productive tropical regions of Australia, India, Borneo, Sumatra, Java and other equatorial areas where fruit is abundant.

Their favorite roost—or camp, as it is called in Australia—is in great spreading banyan trees, where they live in colonies of several hundred to several thousands. In many parts of the tropics a colony of 10,000 is considered a fairly small colony; a colony of 100,000 is about average; but a colony of 200,000 or more is judged rather large.

Unfortunately for those human beings who must live near the roost or the feeding grounds of a flying fox colony, the voices of these bats are quite audible to human ears. The sounds made by flying foxes are not only audible but also harsh, ugly and almost incessant.

Each evening, while it is still daylight, the flying foxes— which all day long have been hanging, head downward, from the twigs and branches of their roost trees—begin to stir. And the moment they begin to stir, they begin to quarrel, screaming in strident voices and even slashing and biting.

Like almost all of their bat-family relatives, flying foxes begin their nightly activities by flapping their wings while they are still hanging by their feet from their roosts. As soon as they have raised their bodies to a horizontal position by flapping in place, they let go of the perch and instantly fly out and up.

In shrieking pandemonium, then, they circle upward by the thousands, the flapping of their great wings adding to the din. In a packed and brawling mass they wheel above the roost trees for many minutes before they settle into a great horizontal column that moves in steady flight, at about twenty-five miles per hour, across the sunset sky.

The entire colony goes first to water. The dark column bends in the air and seems to flow down to the level of the lake or river or pond that serves as their watering place. Head down, each flying fox laps up its drink with its tongue as it skims just above the surface of the water. And here lies danger. For crocodiles wait just under the surface to snatch at hapless flying foxes as they drink. And many flying foxes fly no farther.

But the loss to crocodiles is so slight as to make no noticeable difference in the size of the flying column or in the cacophony of its clamor as the flying foxes move on toward whatever feeding grounds are to be harvested this night.

There is no social organization in a colony of flying foxes, and no actual leaders guide them in the nightly flight. No one knows how they select their feeding grounds. They may find the ripened fruits by their sense of smell, and perhaps they just go to the closest place that smells best. But each bat flies as an individual, without social relation either to its neighbor or to the colony as a whole, so far as anyone can discover. They are simply all going to the same place, and they travel in the same direction at the same time, much as vacationists' cars jam a highway leading to an ocean resort on a hot summer weekend.

Once the flying foxes arrive at the fruit-filled trees where they will feed for the night, their wrangling becomes violent and ugly. Each flying fox attempts to get the ripest fruit in the best location and to oust whoever has it at the moment. They slash at one another with the razor-sharp claws of their free thumbs. They bite one another with their needle-sharp front teeth. Blood flows, and injuries are many. They shriek and cackle and screech and squawk and scream throughout the night.

In the small hours of early morning, the flying foxes return to their home roost. The raucous noises and the slashing battles are continued as each fox jockeys for better sleeping arrangements in the old home trees.

Worn out at last by all the fighting and the feeding and the flying—for the feeding grounds may be as far as twenty or thirty miles away from the roost trees—the colony of flying foxes sinks into sleep and into silence through the bright, hot hours of the tropical day.

And there they hang, by their hind feet, in the meager shelter offered by branches and leaves, exposed to every passer-by and to every vagary of the weather—and they thrive.

Perhaps large lizards and tree snakes prey upon flying foxes as they sleep through the day, but it is not known for certain that they do. Certain kinds of eagles may take them from their trees or as they fly from their roosts in the early evenings, but, again, no one is sure.

We do know that some people eat flying foxes, and those who eat them say they are mild-flavored and delicious, like poultry or rabbits. However, the odor of a flying fox colony is so rank and so foul that not many people are able to get past the smell to capture the flying animals as food.

And it is true that the person who skins a flying fox is extremely careful to prevent the fur from touching the meat. If the fur touches the meat it is said to impart a most unpleasant flavor, so offensive that the meat cannot be eaten. So man does not strike often as a predator of flying foxes. Even fruit growers use nets, instead of traps or poisons, to protect their trees.

Another enemy that strikes but seldom in their habitat is a swift change in temperature, against which, in their exposed roosting, the flying foxes have no protection. Heavy rains and mists seem to cause them little difficulty. They go to their feeding grounds through the wetness with no apparent slackening of interest or numbers. If the weather grows cool during the day—and it does, sometimes, even in the tropics—they crowd closer together and wrap their great wings around their bodies to preserve their body heat. When cold persists through the night, the flying foxes go neither to drink nor to feed, but remain in their roosts. If a cold spell were to continue long in their region, many flying foxes conceivably would starve to death.

Flying foxes also suffer from the heat. On days of high temperature they stay awake through the day, fanning themselves with their wings. Strangely, they do not fan with both wings at the same time but first with one wing and then with the other. This fanning cools their bodies by stirring the air about them, and it also increases heat loss through the network of blood vessels in the thin membranes of their wings. When sudden hot blasts of air sweep through a region, as sometimes happens, flying foxes are seen to fall from their trees to the ground, and many of them die, almost instantly.

The constant and real enemies of flying foxes, as of all bats, are parasitic flies, fleas and mites, which feed on their blood. To combat these small enemies, flying foxes and other bats diligently comb out their fur with the claws of their hind feet, lick their fur to a polish with their tongues, and bite at the little pests with their teeth.

Instead of having just one claw—the thumb claw—free of the wing membrane, flying foxes also have a free claw at the end of the index finger. This second claw is a great advantage to them as they clamber about among the interlaced twigs and branches of the trees on which they feed.

Flying foxes use their wings for grasping almost as much as they use them for flying. Not only do they climb with the aid of their wings, they also hold their food in them. A flying fox alights, upside down, beside a ripened fruit—banana, plum, guava or mango—and, holding it securely against its chest with one wing, it bends its head upward and eats the fruit. At other times, the fox breaks the fruit from its stem and holds it in the fold of a wing, or clasps it between its two wrists while, still upside down, eating the fruit.

Yet to say that the flying fox eats the fruit is not quite exact. What it does is to press bites of the fruit between its flat, smooth-topped molars. By this pressure the fox squeezes the juice down its throat, and spits out the seeds and the pulp. In the case of such fruits as bananas and very ripe guavas it obviously swallows a great deal, perhaps most, of the pulp.

Flying foxes have a habit of bringing some fruit home with them each night from the feeding grounds, "to eat in bed," as it were. They plunge their hind claws into a whole fruit, as though their claws were the tines of a fork, and carry it home in their feet. So many fruit seeds are carried to the home roost in this manner that in parts of India people rent the rights to gather the seeds from beneath the roost trees. (Roost trees, incidentally, are not always banyan trees. They may be almost any kind of tree. Flying foxes often roost in fig trees, in tamarinds and even in bambo.)

Like virtually all their relatives, flying foxes mate in the late autumn, but, as with hibernating bats, conception does not take place until early spring, and the young are born in late spring or early summer.

A baby flying fox is the size of a large mouse—three or four inches long—when it is born. It is blind and helpless, but it usually has just the faintest cover of downy hair. Its feet and its wing claws cling tightly to its mother's fur, its mouth is clamped to one of her nipples, and there the baby lives, fastened securely to its mother's belly, until it is ready to fly on its own wings.

These babies soon become a heavy burden upon their mothers. As the dark column flies across the sky each evening, the slower, labored flying of the mothers may be easily recognized. Every now and then one of the mothers loses her balance and falters in the air as the youngster at her breast lurches to a different position and shifts the weight load without warning. To skim low over the water and lap up her evening drink requires exquisite control, and should the baby alter its station during this maneuver both baby and mother are likely to fall into the water and drown, or be quickly eaten by a lucky crocodile.

For how many weeks a mother flying fox carries her baby to the feeding grounds we do not know, but the youngsters apparently are never left behind at the roosting trees, and they are known to be at the feeding stations when they are scarcely old enough to leave the mother's breast.

When they are about three months old, they are hung by their hind feet to the branch of a tree at the feeding station and left there while the mothers feed. The mothers visit them periodically through the night, bringing them bits of fruit and possibly allowing them to nurse, although this is, quite likely, a time of weaning. The young ones are carried by their mothers to the feeding stations until they are four months old, and even at that age they probably make only parts of the flights to the feeding grounds on their own wings. At eight months of age, although they are quite independent of their mothers, they are still not fully grown.

Because the food of the flying foxes stays in one place and does not have to be pursued through the nighttime air, the foxes fly much more slowly and without the erratic plungings and complicated maneuvers of their insect-eating relatives. The mechanics of their flight, though, are exactly the same. They swim through the air with great, purposeful strokes powered and controlled by their entire bodies, raising folded wings above their backs and sweeping them downward and forward, then upward and back.

But flying foxes navigate by sight and not by hearing. Their ears are simple, and their eyes are large. (A blindfolded flying fox is practically helpless.) They utter few, if any, high-frequency sounds, and they have no special echo-location equipment to translate such signals. Their ears have no tragus or antitragus, nor do foxes have any facial crests around their noses. They do have large and marvelously sensitive wings but, so far as we know, they find their way entirely by sight.

The eye of the flying fox is different from the eye of any other animal. Instead of the retina being smooth, as in other animals, it is made up of a mass of small bulges that are highly sensitive to light. With so much surface on its retina for catching every possible lumen of light, the flying fox is probably able to see extremely well in the dark. But flying foxes do not see perfectly. They often crash into telephone lines and power lines that any insect-eating bat, using its finely tuned echo-location system, would easily avoid.

FLYING SQUIRRELS

Squirrels of the kind that glide about their forested habitats on soft, furry membranes are scattered over most of the world, but not in South America or Australia. Neither are they found in the treeless polar regions, although some flying squirrels in woolly fur coats do live among the lichen-covered rocks in the high, cold countries of Kashmir and Tibet. The largest flying squirrels, three feet long from tip of nose to tip of tail, live in Asia, and the smallest, like tiny gliding mice, live in Africa.

The best known and most studied of all these flying squirrels is the little creature of our own land that the Indians of North America called Assapanick. The scientific world gave it the name *Glaucomys volans*, which means "flying silver-gray mouse." Most of us simply call it the flying squirrel. And, while the habits and life styles of all flying squirrels are much the same, it is specifically this small North American species we shall now investigate.

If you watch an ordinary gray squirrel or red squirrel as it makes a long flying leap from one limb to another, you will see that it spreads its four legs widely apart, that it broadens and flattens its entire body, and that its tail, slightly curved, streams broadly out behind it. All this makes the squirrel as wide and as flat as it can possibly be, and gives its body a great deal of surface, in comparison with its weight, for gliding through the air.

The true flying squirrel, though, is far better equipped for gliding than are these larger relatives of his, and it glides for distances as great as thirty or forty yards. It has a gliding-membrane, or fold of skin, extending from the sides of its body and attached to its arms and legs, so that when the flying squirrel bounds into the air with its legs and arms outstretched, it is spread out like a sheet of paper on the wind. It has a rod of cartilage at each wrist to give this membrane extra support and to help keep it broadly expanded.

When a flying squirrel is ready to take off from its treetop airdrome, it looks carefully down to the spot where it intends to land. It leans to the right and then to the left, then repeats the observation. This is a regular procedure among flying squirrels. Apparently it is measuring, by triangulation, the distance that has to be covered. If the squirrel is frightened into leaping before finishing these observations, it makes a poor flight, either landing on the ground, which it usually tries to avoid doing, or falling in the water, where it will probably drown. (It is badly hampered in water by its gliding-membranes and is one of the few mammals that cannot swim.)

When the flying squirrel completes its apparent measure-

ments, it gathers its four tiny limbs together and gives a mighty spring upward. Spreading legs and arms out as widely as possible, the squirrel stretches its gliding-membrane to its widest and allows it to fill, like a parachute, with the air that is rushing by. This membrane, thin as it is, contains sheets of muscles that can be tensed or relaxed at will, thus making it possible for the little squirrel to change its course as it glides, to avoid twigs, limbs, tree trunks or anything else that gets in its way.

Its fluffy tail is the rudder that guides these turns and provides a strong control in all its landings. As the squirrel nears its chosen spot, it flips its tail straight up in the air. This deflects the head and body upward. At the same time, it reaches forward with both arms and legs, allowing the membranes to curve and fill with air. The squirrel's speed is slowed by this

air-scooping action, and it lands on the trunk of the tree, hind feet first but facing upward, as lightly as a falling leaf.

Instantly, without a second's pause, this gentle and timid little animal scurries around to the other side of the tree. This instinctive action serves to confuse any owl that may have been following, or any cat, raccoon or weasel that may have been watching the flight from below and waiting for the little squirrel to land.

If traveling farther in the woods, the flying squirrel races up the tree and takes off again. But you have to watch closely in order to see this. The little fellow scurries about incredibly fast, so fleet and sure of foot that it is difficult, and sometimes impossible, to see it, even in moonlight.

For it is well after dark when the flying squirrel pops out of its nest and begins its busy life of gliding and eating and drinking. The squirrel is nervous on the ground because of its many predators, but there it must hunt for food and water.

Because it burns energy very fast, the flying squirrel is a huge eater and drinker. It eats berries and fruits and grains, blossoms and leaves and the bark of twigs, seeds and nuts and mushrooms and lichens, insects and birds' eggs and tiny baby birds. And it drinks, each night, almost enough water to float itself.

The flying squirrel is a tiny creature that weighs only two and one-half ounces when fully grown, with a body about five inches long and a tail nearly four inches. Its dense and fine fur is grayish or brownish over its back and a soft, creamy white below. Its head is round, and its eyes are large and dark and liquid.

The flying squirrel chatters much of the time when it is out and about, making a sound somewhat like the gray squirrel's— "chuck, chuck, chuck." When it is angry or alarmed it gives out a series of short, sharp squeals. Sometimes—for its own amusement, apparently—it "sings" in a clear, musical chirping note repeated for minutes at a time. This song sounds like a bird's high twittering except that it often turns harsh and loses its singing quality.

Most of the flying squirrel's life is spent in hardwood trees. It prefers beech and maple, then oak and hickory, beyond all other trees. Its home is usually a hollow limb or a deserted woodpecker hole that it lines with shreds of bark, dry leaves, moss, feathers, fur or whatever soft materials it can find. But it sometimes builds a leaf nest, like that of the gray squirrel, in the crotch of a limb, and it has been known to live underground when a forest fire has destroyed all the trees. But whatever its nest, it is, without fail, situated near a supply of water.

The flying squirrel hoards nuts and seeds for the winter. It keeps a supply in its own nest chamber and hides the rest about in various niches and storage holes in its own territory. While carrying its food in its mouth, it apparently marks it with its own odor, so that its hoard is never appropriated by any of its squirrel relatives.

Several flying squirrels usually live together, sharing the nest, and they sleep curled up in furry balls with their tails fluffed over their round little heads. Twenty or more may den together through the cold winter months.

Flying squirrels do not truly hibernate but, like the gray squirrel and the red, stay snug in the nest through bitterly cold, windy or wet weather. They conserve both energy and body fluids by sleeping deeply during those stormy periods.

Baby flying squirrels are born at any time from early spring through the summer and into September. Each mother usually has two litters during that period, and there are from two to six babies in each litter. They come into the world naked and pink, blind and wrinkled, and each one weighs about one-fifteenth of an ounce—transparent baby-sized gliding-membranes and all.

Their eyes are not fully opened until they are almost one month old; they continue to nurse until they are at least two months old; and they do not begin to glide until they have reached the age of three months. Strangely, until the moment they begin to glide, these young squirrels are not particularly active, and they seem to be quite unsure of themselves in any moving about that they do attempt.

They are unsure about their first gliding attempts, too. No

one teaches them, and they have to work out all the mechanics by themselves. They climb onto a limb and pick out a tree trunk to land upon. Then they rock uncertainly back and forth, back and forth, right and left, up on their toes and down again.

When finally they make their first leaps into the air, they stretch out their gliding-membranes and go gliding swiftly downward. But they usually have trouble with their flight controls, and they find themselves somersaulting through the air, slipping wildly to one side or the other, making belly landings on the ground, or falling short of their intended landing places.

Once started, though, they practice constantly and quickly perfect their gliding skills. From then on, they spend their nights gliding through the forest aisles, finding their own food and water, and learning to escape the teeth and claws of their ever-hungry predators.

EPILOGUE

FLYING INSECTS—
AND THE
COURSE OF EVOLUTION

The ability to fly is a distinct advantage to any living thing. By taking to the air, a creature with wings can easily escape from an earthbound predator, from a flood, or from a forest fire. It can forage for its food over a wide and varied area; it can move from a region of drought and famine to a land of greater plenty, or flee from a northland winter to a summer in the south. And it can expand its search for mates over a larger territory.

So much survival value is concentrated in the power of flight that it may be the course of animal evolution. Perhaps the soaring and gliding creatures described in this book are the forerunners of animals that, in another million years, will fly on splendid wings developed from the gliding-membranes they now have.

The flying insects provide an example of such evolution. Biologists tell us that the first insects to "fly" actually were able only to sail from leaf to leaf or from tall plants down to the ground. Their "wings" were merely stiff, immovable extensions from the sides of their thoraxes.

As eons passed, the insects' gliding-vanes slowly became larger, and they were able to glide for longer distances. Each time these primeval insects sailed through the air, the vanes tended to flutter in the breezes set up by their own passing, and this involuntary fluttering began to develop muscle tissue at the base of the vanes. When, after a million or so years, the insects began to use these muscles a little to move their gliding-vanes up and down in the air, the exercise caused even greater development of the tissues, and the insects gained both increased speed and greater control in flight. In this slow and gradual way, by the selective process known as the survival of the fittest, insects developed the art of flying. They took to the air and had it all to themselves for more than a hundred million years, until the birds appeared to challenge them there.

Birds, however, had to sacrifice their arms in order to fly. They had to grow long, strong feathers on their arms as well as on their tails to give them enough surface to sail upon and to give them the means for controlling their flights.

But the insects sacrificed none of their six fine legs. Instead, they developed two pairs of separate and special organs on which to fly. Butterflies and moths developed the largest wings of any insects. Extremely thin and covered with scales, the hind- and forewings hook together in flight, so that they function as one broad wing. Dragonflies, the champion fliers among the insects, use their slender, glistening wings alternately. When the front wings are down, the back wings are raised. Beetles boast forewings that have hardened into protective wing cases for the chiffonlike rear wings on which the beetles fly. And the wings of mosquitoes and of bees and of the myriad flies are narrow and thin and mostly transparent.

All these diversely modified insect wings are stiffened and supported by the systems of blood veins that transect them, and every wing has the same basic vein pattern. The veins on the leading edges of all insect wings are heavier than the veins on the trailing edges, so, as the wings move forward and down, backward and up, the flexible rear portions of the wings bend, thus giving the necessary forward thrust to the insects' flight.

There are muscles at the base of the wings for the control of many of the motions of flying, but the up-and-down motions of most, and presumably all, insects' wings are powered by two sets of springlike muscles on the thorax. These muscles, once put into motion, work as automatically as the pistons on an engine. As one set of muscles bends the top of the thorax down, the wings are forced up and the opposite set of muscles is stretched. At the end of the pull, the first set of muscles relaxes and the second set takes over, bending the top of the thorax up, pulling the wings down, and stretching the first set of muscles again. Thus it becomes an automatic give-and-take of power between the two sets of flight muscles.

Because this motion is automatic and not the result of nerve stimulation, as in birds, insect wings can beat extremely fast. And only because insect wings can beat so fast can such insects as bumblebees, with bulky bodies and skimpy wings, fly at all.

Both the bumblebee and the honeybee beat their wings 250 times per second, the housefly 190 times, the hornet 100 times; while the rapidly vibrating wings of the hummingbird, for comparison, only beat 30 to 50 times per second. And the little midge dancing in the air beats its wings at 1,000 times per second.

For their size, insects can fly at amazing speeds. A dragonfly exceeds fifteen miles per hour, and even the drifting swallowtail butterfly does nearly six miles per hour. They can fly great distances and climb thousands of feet up into the air. They can twist and turn, dart and dash, zigzag and spin, and take off and land with most remarkable agility.

Some insects, like the whirligigs, backswimmers and water striders, spend most of their lives at or on the surface of the water, but they can also dive into its depths or they can spread their wings and fly above it. These insects keep their wings closely folded and out of the way when they are submerged. But the tiny fairy fly, who lays her eggs within the underwater eggs of the dragonfly, takes the best of both worlds, using her wings not only for flying in the air but also for swimming under the water.

And all this present-day diversity and skill in the art of flying came about in the insect world because, several hundreds of millions of years ago, their ancestral forms developed gliding-vanes that, little by little, enabled them to increase the size of their feeding and mating territories and enhanced their chances of survival.

The gliding-membranes of the flying frogs, flying lizards, flying marsupials, flying lemurs and flying squirrels of today are likewise responsible for extending the territory over which these creatures can feed. Their ability to glide also helps them to escape from such enemies as the predatory snakes and birds that they meet in their treetop habitats.

How gliding-membranes developed in these animals we do not know, because the fossil-bearing rocks show no trace of the soft tissue of those membranes, unlike the hard gliding-vanes of the insects, which left their history there. Perhaps, in the beginning, these soft membranes were only the faintest extensions of skin along an animal's sides. But even this faint strip of skin enabled the animal to leap just a little farther, and so it increased the animal's chances of survival, however slightly. The tendency to develop this strip of skin was passed on to the animal's offspring, and, because the projections gave advantages to those who possessed them, through millenniums of time they grew larger and larger until they reached the sizes we see today. These membranes still have great survival value, and the creatures endowed with them use them gracefully and continuously, able to control their soaring descents and subsequent landings to a considerable degree.

If the faintest beginnings of flight-muscle tissues are now developing on the shoulders and sides of these gliding animals, we cannot discover them. But if the mere involuntary fluttering of stiff vanes once developed muscles for insect flight, perhaps the intentional spreading, flexing and folding of these soft membranes will, in several millions of years to come, also develop flight muscles for these animals.

More than flight muscles are needed, of course. With their development, skeletal changes such as the hollowing of the bones will have to take place. Alterations to the animal's general body shape might occur, and, quite probably, transformations in its brain as well, to give quick control over motion and balance. For passing through the air creates its own engineering problems.

When we look at the webbing in the feet and hands of flying frogs, we wonder if this was how the wings of bats began. Will the hand bones and finger bones of these frogs elongate and the areas of webbing expand as, over the course of millions of years, the frogs continue to glide through the air?

What, possibly, may become of the flying snake in a hundred years? Or of the flying fish? Will the gray squirrel and the red squirrel, which now extend their leaps and soften their falls by flattening and spreading their bodies, develop gliding-membranes in another million years? And, perhaps, wings in a hundred million?

It does not seem likely that people will ever develop wings or the ability to fly powered by their own muscles. They have, instead, developed machines to carry them through the air— airplanes and helicopters, gliders and hang gliders, balloons and zeppelins and parachutes and kites. They climb aboard or fasten themselves to these various inventions, and, barring accident or adverse weather, they bring under their own control the distance, direction and destination of their flight, just as the insects, the bats and the birds do.

Given another hundred million years, people will certainly develop even more marvelous machines and amazing methods for getting from here to there, but they will continue to look with envy upon all the animals with wings—and wish, as Icarus in the Greek legend wished, that they, too, could truly fly.

METRIC MEASUREMENTS BIBLIOGRAPHY

METRIC MEASUREMENTS

Flying fish (family Exocoetidae, several genera, several species)
LENGTH: 150–450 mm

Flying hatchetfish or characin (*Gasteroplecus*, several species)
LENGTH: 25–65 mm; TAKEOFF RUN: 12 m; GLIDE: 125–250 mm

Butterfly fish (*Pantodon buchholzi*)
LENGTH: 125 mm

Flying gurnard (*Dactylopterus volitans*)
LENGTH: 300 mm

Flying frog (*Rhacophorus*, several species)
LENGTH: female—75 mm, male—50 mm; GLIDE: 10 m, 30–40 m max.

Flying lizards:

Flying dragon (*Draco volans*)
LENGTH: 300–400 mm

Flying gecko (*Ptychozoon homalocephalum*)
LENGTH: 200 mm

Flying snake (*Chrysopelea ornata*)
LENGTH: approx. 1 m

Flying marsupials:

Feathertail glider (*Acrobates pygmaeus*)
HEAD AND BODY: 60–80 mm; TAIL: 65–80 mm; WEIGHT:
female of 73 mm (head and body)—12 gm, male of 75
mm—14 gm

Sugar or honey glider (*Petaurus breviceps*), **squirrel glider**
(*Petaurus norfolcensis*), **yellow-bellied glider** (*Petaurus
australis*)
HEAD AND BODY: 120–320 mm; TAIL: 150–480 mm; WEIGHT:
female of 163 mm (head and body)—90 gm, male of 163
mm—130 gm; GLIDE: 55 m

Dusky or greater glider (*Schoinobates volans*)
HEAD AND BODY: 300–480 mm; TAIL: 450–550 mm; WEIGHT:
female of 440 mm (head and body)—1.36 kg; GLIDE: 100
mm or more

Flying lemur (*Cynocephalus variegatus*)
HEAD AND BODY: 380–600 mm; TAIL: 220–270 mm; WEIGHT:
1.00–1.75 kg; GLIDE: 136 m or more, losing 10.5–12.0 m elevation

Bat (U.S.) (order Chiroptera)
LENGTH OF FOREARM FROM ELBOW TO WRIST: 30–79 mm;
WEIGHT: 5–65 gm

Flying fox (*Pteropus*, several species)
HEAD AND BODY: approx. 400 mm; LENGTH OF FOREARM FROM
ELBOW TO WRIST: approx. 228 mm; WINGSPAN: 1.00–1.75 m;
WEIGHT: approx. 900 gm

Flying squirrel (*Glaucomys volans*)
HEAD AND BODY: 125–150 mm; TAIL: 90–125 mm; WEIGHT:
50–80 gm; GLIDE: 50 m, at rate of 22 m in 12 sec.

BIBLIOGRAPHY

FLYING FISH

Aistrop, Jack. *Enjoying Nature's Marvels.* New York: Vanguard Press, 1961.

Breland, Osmond P. *Animal Life and Lore.* New York: Harper & Row, 1963.

Herald, Earl S. *Living Fishes of the World.* Garden City, N.Y.: Doubleday & Co., 1961.

Larousse Encyclopedia of Animal Life, The. New York: McGraw-Hill Book Co., 1967.

Marshall, N. B. *Exploration in the Life of Fishes.* Cleveland, O.: World Publishing Co., 1971.

_____. *The Life of Fishes.* Cleveland, O.: World Publishing Co., 1966.

National Geographic Book of Fishes, The. Edited by John Oliver LaGorce. Washington, D.C.: National Geographic Society, 1961.

Seeley, H. G. *Dragons of the Air.* New York: Dover Publications, 1967.

Wallace, Alfred Russel. *The Malay Archipelago.* New York: Dover Publications, 1962.

FLYING FROGS

Boulenger, E. G. *Reptiles and Batrachians.* New York: E. P. Dutton & Co., 1914.

Breland, Osmond P. *Animal Life and Lore.* New York: Harper & Row, 1963.

Cochran, Doris M. *Living Amphibians of the World.* Garden City, N.Y.: Doubleday & Co., 1961.

Larousse Encyclopedia of Animal Life, The. New York: McGraw-Hill Book Co., 1967.

Seeley, H. G. *Dragons of the Air*. New York: Dover Publications, 1967.

Smyth, H. Rucker. *Amphibians and Their Ways*. New York: The Macmillan Co., 1962.

Wallace, Alfred Russel. *The Malay Archipelago*. New York: Dover Publications, 1962.

FLYING LIZARDS

Boulenger, E. G. *Reptiles and Batrachians*. New York: E. P. Dutton & Co., 1914.

Ditmars, Raymond L. *Reptiles of the World*. New York: The Macmillan Co., 1933.

Earle, Olive L. *Strange Lizards*. New York: William Morrow & Co., 1964.

Larousse Encyclopedia of Animal Life, The. New York: McGraw-Hill Book Co., 1967.

McMichael, D. F., ed. *A Treasury of Australian Wildlife*. New York: Taplinger Publishing Co., 1968.

Orr, Robert T. *The Animal Kingdom*. New York: The Macmillan Co., 1965.

Pope, Clifford H. *The Reptile World*. New York: Alfred A. Knopf, 1955.

———. *Reptiles round the World*. New York: Alfred A. Knopf, 1957.

Sanderson, Ivan T. *Investigating the Unexplained*. Englewood Cliffs, N.J.: Prentice-Hall, 1972.

Seeley, H. G. *Dragons of the Air*. New York: Dover Publications, 1967.

FLYING SNAKES

Boulenger, E. G. *Reptiles and Batrachians*. New York: E. P. Dutton & Co., 1914.

Ditmars, Raymond L. *Reptiles of the World*. New York: The Macmillan Co., 1933.

———. *Strange Animals I Have Known*. New York: Harcourt, Brace & Co., 1931.

Larousse Encyclopedia of Animal Life, The. New York: McGraw-Hill Book Co., 1967.

Minton, Sherman A., and Rutherford, Madge. *Venomous Reptiles*. New York: Charles Scribner's Sons, 1969.

Orr, Robert T. *The Animal Kingdom*. New York: The Macmillan Co., 1965.

Parker, H. W. *Natural History of Snakes*. London: British Museum of Natural History, 1965.

Pope, Clifford H. *The Reptile World*. New York: Alfred A. Knopf, 1955.

Sherman, Jane. *The Real Book about Snakes*. Garden City, N.Y.: Garden City Books, 1955.

Stidworthy, John. *Snakes of the World*. New York: Grosset & Dunlap, 1971.

FLYING MARSUPIALS

Barrett, Charles. *An Australian Animal Book*. London: Oxford University Press, 1955.

Bourlière, François. *The Natural History of Mammals*. New York: Alfred A. Knopf, 1964.

Grzimek, Bernhard. *Four-Legged Australians*. New York: Hill & Wang, 1967.

Larousse Encyclopedia of Animal Life, The. New York: McGraw-Hill Book Co., 1967.

Morris, Desmond. *The Mammals*. New York: Harper & Row, 1965.

Prince, J. H. *Animals in the Night*. New York: Thomas Nelson, 1971.

Sanderson, Ivan T. *Living Mammals of the World*. Garden City, N.Y.: Doubleday & Co., 1975.

Scott, Jack Denton. *Speaking Wildly*. New York: William Morrow & Co., 1966.

Troughton, Ellis. *Furred Animals of Australia*. Narbeth, Pa.: Livingston Publishing Co., 1966.

Walker, Ernest P. *Mammals of the World*. 3d ed. Vol. 1. Baltimore: The Johns Hopkins University Press, 1975.

Whitley, Gilbert P.; Brodie, C. F.; Morcombe, M. K.; and Kinghorn, J. R. *Animals of the World—Australia* (n.p., n.d.).

FLYING LEMURS

Larousse Encyclopedia of Animal Life, The. New York: McGraw-Hill Book Co., 1967.

Morris, Desmond. *The Mammals*. New York: Harper & Row, 1965.

Orr, Robert T. *The Animal Kingdom*. New York: The Macmillan Co., 1965.

Sanderson, Ivan T. *Living Mammals of the World*. Garden City, N. Y.: Doubleday & Co., 1975.

Seeley, H. G. *Dragons of the Air.* New York: Dover Publications, 1967.
Walker, Ernest P. *Mammals of the World.* 3d ed. Vol. 1. Baltimore: The Johns Hopkins University Press, 1975.
Wallace, Alfred Russel. *The Malay Archipelago.* New York: Dover Publications, 1962.

BATS

Anthony, Harold E. *Mammals of America.* Garden City, N.Y.: Garden City Publishing Co., 1937.
Barker, Will. *Familiar Animals of America.* New York: Harper & Bros., 1956.
Bourlière, François. *The Natural History of Mammals.* New York: Alfred A. Knopf, 1964.
Burton, Maurice. *The Sixth Sense of Animals.* New York: Taplinger Publishing Co., 1973.
Larousse Encyclopedia of Animal Life, The. New York: McGraw-Hill Book Co., 1967.
May, Charles Paul. *Bats.* New York: Meredith Press, 1969.
Morris, Desmond. *The Mammals.* New York: Harper & Row, 1965.
Orr, Robert T. *The Animal Kingdom.* New York: The Macmillan Co., 1965.
Seeley, H. G. *Dragons of the Air.* New York: Dover Publications, 1967.
Walker, Ernest P. *Mammals of the World.* 3d ed. Vol. 1. Baltimore: The Johns Hopkins University Press, 1975.

FLYING FOXES

Aistrop, Jack. *Enjoying Nature's Marvels.* New York: Vanguard Press, 1961.
Barrett, Charles. *An Australian Animal Book.* London: Oxford University Press, 1955.
Bourlière, François. *The Natural History of Mammals.* New York: Alfred A. Knopf, 1964.
Larousse Encyclopedia of Animal Life, The. New York: McGraw-Hill Book Co., 1967.
May, Charles Paul. *Bats.* New York: Meredith Press, 1969.
Morris, Desmond. *The Mammals.* New York: Harper & Row, 1965.
Prince, J. H. *Animals in the Night.* New York: Thomas Nelson, 1971.

Sanderson, Ivan T. *Living Mammals of the World*. Garden City, N.Y.: Doubleday & Co., 1975.
Walker, Ernest P. *Mammals of the World*. 3d ed. Vol. 1. Baltimore: The Johns Hopkins University Press, 1975.

FLYING SQUIRRELS

Barker, Will. *Familiar Animals of America*. New York: Harper & Bros., 1956.
Bourlière, François. *The Natural History of Mammals*. New York: Alfred A. Knopf, 1964.
Dodd, Ed. "Mark Trail." *The Baltimore Sun*, 13 August 1972.
Grzimek, Bernhard. *Four-Legged Australians*. New York: Hill & Wang, 1967.
Larousse Encyclopedia of Animal Life, The. New York: McGraw-Hill Book Co., 1967.
Prince, J. H. *Animals in the Night*. New York: Thomas Nelson, 1971.
Sanderson, Ivan T. *Living Mammals of the World*. Garden City, N.Y.: Doubleday & Co., 1975.
Walker, Ernest P. *Mammals of the World*. 3d ed. Vol. 2. Baltimore: The Johns Hopkins University Press, 1975.

INSECTS—AND THE COURSE OF EVOLUTION

Ebert, James D.; Loewy, Ariel G.; Miller, Richard S.; and Schneiderman, Howard A. *E.L.M.S. Biology*. New York: Holt, Rinehart and Winston, 1973.
Encyclopaedia Britannica, Vol. 12: "Insects." Chicago: Encyclopaedia Britannica, 1943.
Fuller, Harry J., and Carothers, Zane B. *The Plant World*. New York: Holt, Rinehart and Winston, 1963.
Headstrom, Richard. *Nature in Miniature*. New York: Alfred A. Knopf, 1968.
"How Insects Fly." *Time*, 12 September 1960.
Hutchins, Ross E. *Insects*. Englewood Cliffs, N.J.: Prentice-Hall, 1966.

Designed by Barbara Holdridge

Composed in Century Schoolbook by Service Composition Company, Baltimore, Maryland, with West Nouveau Didot display by Photo Lettering, Inc., New York, New York

Color separation by Graphic Technology, Fort Lauderdale, Florida

Printed on 70-lb. Mead Moistrite Opaque Offset, Regular Finish, by Science Press, Ephrata, Pennsylvania

Bound in Kivar Corinthian Gray and Kivar Renaissance Emerald Green by the Delmar Printing Company, Charlotte, North Carolina